# In New Jersey

## By Julie Ellinger Hunt

ISBN 978-1-936373-14-7

Published in the United States by Unbound Content, LLC, Englewood, NJ.
Cover art: Joyful ©2010, by Julie Ellinger Hunt.
The poems in this collection are all original and previously unpublished with the exception of those listed in the credits page at the end of the volume.

*In*

*New Jersey*

First edition 2011

**unbound CONTENT**

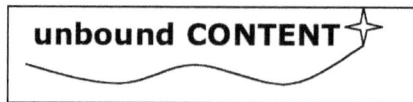

*For my dad for always pushing me harder and loving me furiously. For my stepmother for always rooting me on. For my mother who told me that no matter what, I was special. For my husband for putting up with a poet's weird moods and loving me anyway. And for my precious sons: your patience while I write is remarkable, just like my love for you.*

—Julie Ellinger Hunt

# Table of Contents

# THERE

## SOMEWHERE ELSE

## Introduction

Sure, you've heard the jokes about the Turnpike and the hair, you've laughed at the accent and loved the tomatoes, you've even been to both Philly and Manhattan. But have you really been to New Jersey?

Until you've gone down the shore (and told someone about it) you don't know why pizza is better with sand on it. Until you've gone to a feast (not a street fair), you don't know that a zeppole is as close to heaven as you'll ever get. Until you've taken the 168 bus to Port Authority, you can't know why it makes sense that Alfred Kinsey (yes, the sexologist) was raised here.

Jersey hair is not about hairspray. It's about humidity, windows-down driving, and gel. The Jersey accent is not about coffee. It's about the language and cadences of Philip Roth, Junot Diaz, Anne Morrow Lindbergh, and William Carlos Williams.

Haven't spent much time here? Then sit down for a conversation with Julie Ellinger Hunt, as genuine a Jersey girl as you'll ever meet. Listen to her musings on love, art, and life. Acquaint yourself with the lilt of her voice. Visit her landscapes, interior as well as exterior. Do this and you will know a little better the nature of this mythical and much maligned place. It isn't Oz, and it certainly isn't Kansas, but it's a place as vast and limitless as if it were bordered by rainbows and prairies and the ceiling of the plane-tracked sky.

—Annmarie Lockhart
editor, vox poetica

# HERE

## In New Jersey

Day One:

I dreamt I had six legs and no heartbeat. I was walking backward singing the song my mother sang to me. I gagged when I awoke. Shuffled swiftly toward the bathroom and greeted my porcelain king. He obliged and lent me his soul. I always had too much wine when I was lonely.

Day Two:

So you came to visit. The sun lingered longer that mid-afternoon. We ate popsicles and danced with fireflies. You lent me your favorite book and rubbed my back until I fell asleep. You told me my eyelids fluttered a bit which made you nervous. I fell in love with you when you said that, even though you laughed at me.

Day Three:

Tom Waits is your hero. I can hardly stand him but I'm learning about compromise. I compromised to tolerate Tom Waits on every other Tuesday. That made you give me the "pfffft" laugh I love so much. Before I know it, my clothes are off and we're back in high school form. I want to write your name all over my body. You threaten to take me to prom. I remind you that I am trying to stay away from my porcelain king.

All you say is "ha."

Day Four:

A bird took a huge shit on my car. We all know that's normal, but for me to look at that shit and see something that can't be there?! Now that's insanity. It dripped down the side and formed a perfect heart. Afraid to offend love or something stupid, I leave it be. Now I'm stuck with shit.

Day Five:

I closed my eyes and when they opened I saw your face so I sketched it. It's an uncanny drawing since I don't draw that well. It really looks like you. I'll hide it and give it to you sometime.

Day Six:

We met in Morristown. You ordered either a buffalo or Cajun chicken sandwich. Your rainbow eyes danced a bit when you smiled. Little did I know how much that smile would do to me.

<u>Year One:</u>

Plans cannot be promised, you say, but I feel they will come. Sure, I'm half human and you're full superb. And you think it's the other way around, which makes you even more superb. You say very little. Most people would be annoyed. But not me. Your expression speaks just fine. And it says things you never will . . . even when we're old and haggard and I'm begging you to clean the bird shit off the porch.

*Appeared first at* The Momo Reader.

## Hudson County Girl

I used to live right across the river
on the New Jersey side—
Manhattan and Guttenberg like kissing
cousins,
West New York, a close sentimental lover.

I'd walk the line on the exaggerated cliffs
on my own,
the loner I fought to be
while pretty girls tend to have a small following.
Notebook always in hand—

I'd write gibberish high school woes
that seemed immensely important
to a fifteen-year-old always moving,
always trying to keep outsiders at
arm's length.

It was near that river
I fell apart and scattered all around
Hudson County
then healed
then fell apart again . . .

the standard cycle of a typical
American teenager trying to make
sense of herself and the enormous
world that awaited.

*Appeared first at* vox poetica.

## 2: A Demonstrative Tempest

My skin left me today.
Decided it was stretched too thin,
absurdly expected to clothe two people.
It was sick of being shared.

A lilac breeze triggered one of me to
let go of your face in my head, so I
did, ash embers spread to a neighbor's
flowerbed. She swept it away before
it smoldered.

Pavement footsteps echoed retreat.
Two people divided yet whole.
Separate, different. Unaware of
the fight to survive on their own
without the counter part looming,
ready to pounce back aside.

Under an old vacant shed, buried
in rock and debris a faded
cardboard box held both of me.
In aged time . . . cleverly compostable.

Without skin to bind us together
or fear to keep us aligned, I finally
sensed the beauty of it all. Why two
must exist in one. The mother to the
fighter. The woman to the believer.
The core to the outskirts . . . but all
human. All noble and compulsory
to survive a demonstrative tempest.

*Appeared first at* Rafter.

## Wild Neighborhood

Impatient legs strolling.
Circles running wild.
Tree roots up-root, tons
of barked men run naked
moonlights walkways nowadays
sprinklers explode in unison
a robin's egg falls from its nested
bed. A bed of moss births mushroom
caps. The stems still beneath.
a sewer grate unhinges and rolls
away like tumbleweed.

I, alas, am only an observer

in the wild neighborhood.


*Appeared first at* The Momo Reader *and later at* Instigatorzine.

## In My Hand

There's a cling-clanging below, the sun
falls behind a cloud again.
A ten speed rickets by with little clicks.
A faint pop then another click.
My son grabs the day by its ass. And
shouts, "You are my castle!"
His sword, a stick once buried in the dirt, now his lance,
his rightful weapon.
The little menace is now armed.
Smiles deviously, lunges toward the air-beast.
"I will defeat you!" The lance pierces the wind's heart.

Gavin, now the victor, grabs a fistful of dirt, pours it into
my hand.
My hand, like a sifter, holds onto the crushed
up organs as the blood crumbs flake away.

## July

Outside, rain falls hard. Muffled cars drive fast
avoiding wet acid pellets beating on streets and
walkways. Inside the children wait, rowdy and restless,
resenting nature's cruel playtime interruption.

Here, writing but really hiding, I put everything I can
out of my mind. The river by your house, now cresting,
wreaks havoc in your neighborhood. I keep my distance
for as long as I need to. Rain pounding in my ears
will eventually drown you out some so I can sleep.

## Your Road

I'm like the only car on this road.
It's dark, ridden with shards of glass,
the skeletons of my past, the ashes of
potential days I could have spent with you.
My sick bag of bones I carry, lay in the trunk
and with each bump, they shift and
I become someone new.

This time the dark road is you,
your body, the depths of you.
And I choose to drive onward because
I can finally let my guard down,
breathe normally, take off the costume
I was made to wear, and just drive.

I fell in love with that road
not because it was safe or easy but
because I belonged there. I finally
belonged some place where
I could move forward and understand
how I work. And finally be happy.

As I drove, there were warnings,
flashes, telling me I needed to be
cautious and I didn't see them, I just
drove, tunnel-visioned. I drove on
determined it was my place to navigate,
until you put up that final road block.
And let me go.

Now I can't even figure out how to
make the engine turn . . .

And I'm stuck.

. . . stuck here in this dirt pit.

*Appeared first at* vox poetica.

## A Good Day

My window open slightly, birds' songs
seep through to my bedroom.

The jack hammer up the street finally
takes a coffee break and all the eager canines
are at peace.

A faint plane lingers above my roof—
heading to where planes go. Cars
lull past without hesitation.

I stretch my body toward
the sky, each finger tip reaches
through fragile air.
I breathe in the
paper stacks and globs of ink . . .
I am totally alive.

Refreshed, renewed, refocused . . .

so I write this. It's a good day.

## A Name

A name put forth on a page
detest the clouded ink.
For a name is just as simple as
the light,
while it educates the unknown dark.
And breaks apart from other names
'til it's on its own,
a separate piece.

Will this name be yours or take the
shape of another,
and then disappear as if it was never
muttered in the first place?

Put forth on this page is merely hope
that there will be a name at all.
And I shall have the privilege to know it.
To say it.
To scribe it.
To own it.

## No Longer Color Blind

With eyes closed
the world blanketed
color drained
symbols buried
listening to my own heartbeat
sounds outside start to fade
colors fade too.
I start to fade and then pull back
through orange specks.
I see you
or is it a different you
a part of myself
on this string
pulled then pushed
then dropped.
I pause and take another breath
breathe in the cool blue air
that was once sucked dry.

Eyes now open
the world exposed
colors dance
symbols come through
like wave lengths
my heart slows down
while the orange specks mate
with all the reds and blues and yellows
of my world.
I then see you, it is definitely you!
I pull the string you're anchored by
my arms outstretched
you are now received
the air glows with
rainbow beams
it's me and you,

and we're finally home.

## Sewn Inside Your Jacket

With invisible threads, I'm sewn inside your jacket.
Battered through the weather of you
the whimsical girl on your arm
whistles as my teeth chatter.

The hole near the elbow allows in cold air,
heartbeats slow down to match her pace,
with no warmth, only the black heart
she wants you to wear.

I'm far from her ways,
twisted and tormented, I over analyze,
over worry, over think.
Maybe that's how you got over me.

Never mind the questions I'd bury you
with. The lucidity. The powder keg.
The wine I'd over drink.
The lessons I'd never learn.

My suitcases are always packed.
I'd try to escape and end up
back where I started.
Sewn inside your jacket
next to the black heart I hate.

## Cicadas

The window opened slightly, with barely a breeze I wait.
I hear a distant call from early morning cicadas.
A rise and fall of chirping song, they call to one another
in rattles and buzzes, awkward vibrations.
A simple testimony to their simple requests.

I lay here. While waiting, you enter my mind more than
you should and I can see your uncanny smile, eyes lit up,
embarrassed gazes. You knowing we don't belong in
each other's lives. You, now removed,
have moved on, onward toward sensible things,
a real life I cannot provide for you.
The shame I made you feel is now etched inside me.
Like an inside-out tattoo I wear so you're never too far away.

The cicadas are calling out.
They don't bother with the trivial sentiments we fill our
ears with. Wasted words unaccepted by the few we
want acceptance from. They aren't as desperate to be
heard so much as they are programmed to call out.
I am programmed too,
to keep calling without words,
to keep this song alive within . . .
to rattle and buzz the awkward vibration
of your name over and over,
only it's in my mind and no one can hear me but you.

*Julie Ellinger Hunt*

## Grounded

*The sky can't fall*, I say to myself
as we lie underneath.
We make shadows on the lawn
like a ghost's imprint
and wait for an invisible
wall that divides us.

Next to me, you drift,
possibly asleep, possibly dreaming
of things that make sense, knowing good and well
that I don't. Circling above is a cloud
and in that cloud is me, well, part of me,
the part that isn't grounded here.

## Faucet

I hear the faucet dripping
and in song it tells me to
shut my eyes so I try

a waterfall for tiny beings
or a drink that invisible
monsters devour

a subtle
drip, plop, splat
then it stops
when the wind comes
and drowns it out

but it is still there, dripping

even if it goes unheard


(reminds me of you)

## He Walks at Night

He walks at night in just a trench coat
and battered shoes. He waits until most
are asleep so he may have the streets to
himself. People rarely understand him.

He walks at night in a steady march
and keeps his chin level with the ground.
The dogs sometimes bark but usually it's
quiet. Usually, he brings a can of beer.

Odd men do odd things, he thinks, so he doesn't
fight his nighttime urge to meander. The weather is
docile. Forgiving. So he may walk without strain or
excessive sweat beads building on his hair line.
The can of beer has sweat beads but he welcomes
those, and he tugs on its rough opening every few yards.
Hands shake a bit but he manages fine.

He walks down Pleasant Hill Road but always stays
on the opposite side of the street from the elementary
school.

The school brings him back to his youth and he doesn't
like that.

Under his trench coat is just a pair of boxers his
wife had ironed with a pleat down the middle. He
never understood why she insisted on ironing his
underwear but never protested. Now that she's
gone, he's down to his last pair and he'll miss
that pointless pleat.

But at least now he can get some peace and quiet.
Enjoy his can of beer when he feels like it.
Watch life around him as he sees it.
Walk at night and not worry anyone.

## I Breathed You in Tonight

I breathed you in today when you were asleep.
I finally got to sleep because I felt you near.
Even if you were snoring loudly.

The kids were calm and quiet. The house was still.
I waited til your eyes opened up to tell you I was glad
to have you beside me. Glad to have you home.

Even when I don't say it, I feel it.
Even when you don't feel it, it's true.
I should say it more, I know, but
I really do love you . . .

So tonight, it's ordinary, sure, but
this time, I'm gonna make sure you know
that you're not ordinary. But extraordinary.

That you're pretty damn neat. And I like waking up
next to you . . . even if you do snore most of the night.

## So Yesterday

So yesterday, unlike our normal tryst,
lips purposely held open, like envious petals
open to the sun.
Skin to skin, with warmth generating the perfect heat,
tangled up in one another like a magnetic puzzle,
bodies drawn then stuck with frail but determined
friction.

Black covers hover over us, as we lay, or dance.
Turned around by you, with you, while you are in me.
A ballet of sorts…
and I'm spun just right.
My mind now yours to play in.

## I Wait

In my once beautiful shell, now
haggard and faded, I lay still
and wait.

I wait for you to come and
take me home. Display me on the mantel
that you adorn with pretty things . . . and
watch as they sparkle for you.

I won't sparkle much . . . not for a while . . .
I hope . . . in wait . . .
that spark in me is not
extinguished,
not for good anyway.
That the light beneath my skin will glow
again
my lungs will fill with
solemn air and give new life to worn-out
days
        make my armor shine and leave
        the dullness to rainy days where it belongs.

## In Cups

So I awoke. My hands no longer there,
replaced by cups.
Cups that can hold wine.
Since there was no bracing myself while I stood,
and I was already drunk, wobble-bodied,
I walked the ceiling where the floor ought to be.

And when the door shut behind me, it actually opened.
Its sound, that of a closing door.
The creaking whines made a light flicker but
the flicker was the darkness covering me.
Static shocked, stained by blood I poured as milk, my feet
clung to that ceiling while my head spun off my body.

I was now in two places. One of me clung to the walls
that were already crumbled, while the other paced
the thick air like the moth as it slows before death.
Wings fanning frequently . . . slow until they are only a line
across its body. My body, now two, squares off as
time mirrors space. Space no longer a part of a room

or that in which I exist. I only existed twice. Once for you.
And once for the cups I fill to drink.

## the war raged on

And so the war raged on.
In pink ribbon and sweet sweat
I bowed down before a plastic Buddha statue.
It followed me afterwards, secretly wishing I could
turn him back to gold.
*I'm impotent!* I told him. He just belly-laughed.
*My fibers are just as generic!* He winked.
And so the war raged on.

I poured another glass of wine.
In blue ribbon and tired eyes
kneeled down to wipe the dribble
off the linoleum floor. It smelled
delicious! Fusion of berries, wood,
time and subtlety. Glass full for one
last swig before bed. Yet I wanted more . . .
And so the war raged on.

I only mention this because my mind's
journal was too full of crap to consider
sleep, the plastic Buddha would
have it that I be dead rather than dig
for gold but that war too shall end
in bloodshed and the cable will most likely
go out. I'll have to resort to candlelight and
thumb twiddling.

So the war raged on.

*In New Jersey*

## Paint Thinner

beside an empty box
in shabby arms and
wooden skin
a half a heart beats
or is it a fist clenching tighter
the mist rolls into the living
room so our faces are blurred
like trains passing each other
at top speeds

seeing things after inhaling
paint thinner
dried paint on walls drips
down while I melt
inside you as you
form a barrier in me

stunned from headlights
stung by hornets

while listening to Joan Jett
and scribbling in pink notebooks

Aphrodite is in my mother's closet
Aphrodite is in my swollen womb

half a heart of fist is clenched
then left open
beside an empty box I put
away for now . . .

## Pleasantries

Reflecting in a bay window, outstretched,
calm, collected. Thunderous convulsions and then
release back into a bean-shaped ball. Next door
the wind was howling through a second-story vent
then drowned by a bargain sub-woofer won on eBay.
Mom bangs clumsily on stubborn soil, the last tulip
bulb fighting containment.

Boy in each hand, I walk to my own Central Park.
In mind, the ducks are waiting to be fed day-old bread
and the vagrants wave as my boys' sweet faces swell
smiles then gesture back.

A row of invisible cyclists rushes by.
The local theater just let out and make-believe-
amateur critics are arguing aloud about plot
and ineffective dialogue.

A neighbor's dog escapes the fence and
nuzzles my leg with his wet nose.

My son giggles at the mime I imagine.
Pretends he's sliding down a magic
escalator and then pulls a balloon
animal from his top hat.

I imagine it's an elaborate poodle with a wet nose.

Fused with suburban slight
and urban frustration, I get
lost on our walk home trying
to look for my very own Serendipity.

## Sun Set

The sun set a little funny today so I thought of you.
Your crooked smile, my crooked emotions. Your
reaction to my crooked emotions.

We didn't get a chance to laugh together
this week so maybe
that's why the sun looked funny.
Maybe it hovered longer so the shadows
could linger longer.
The way shadows dance in your eyes
is like magic. There's a lot of magic around you
but you haven't the faintest clue.

Maybe that is magic in itself.

We agreed to a world with no god,
no divine meanings
and yet I cannot explain any of this. How I'm
drawn to you like the crazy bugs race to the
fluorescent light above my back door . . .
How I can see your thoughts as I can see
my own . . . finish sentences you have not
started to say.

The hairs on the back of your neck stood
high at exactly 1:04 pm.
I noticed 38 miles away.
            By the way
      is there even a way
any of this could happen?

*Dissection, analysis and worry aren't*
*accomplishing much so let it be,* I say
to myself and to you. And to myself
over again. It's not like either of
us to leave things alone with no further
study.

One less sunset for me to watch
alone I hope. Another day
together. When I know my head
voices can wrestle less. Rest more.

I sift through words in my head
but none will do at this moment
to finish this thought other than these:
I'm in awe of you.

## Wrapped in Brown Paper

Wrapped in brown paper cut from
grocery bags, all thumbs . . . but kept tidy
      still edges, clean of the black ink left
      aside for the address label . . . born
      from dirty thoughts and
      sleeplessness, boredom too.

Tragedy struck the neighbor-
hood twice in one month. Left balled
      up cans in foundation cracks, litter
      collected in curb-side clusters.

Under an awning the package
sits and waits for
      postal pickup while a child
      quietly whistles a tune in
      harmony with a roaring garbage
      truck.

Rain plays in cascades on worn
out roof tops . . . tickling shingles.

Bade on youth for stronger wrists
grip and tie down. Hold and conquer.
      The package leaves the porch for good.
      It whispers goodbye in paper tongue.
      It leaves behind a dry spot under the
      awning while rain spews in sideways.

## Plastic Bubbles With Trinkets Inside

When I was four, I thought plastic bubbles
with trinkets inside were as valuable
as King Tut's tomb—
Our housekeeper would say:
*tesoros están en nuestros ojos*
and I'd swoon at the possibility
that my eyes were gems
or that the world may hold
something in the tiny crevices
that normally held dust bunnies.

I'd look at things differently—
in a way we lose when we age.
Reveling at a 25-cent plastic
bubble with something so
trivial inside.

Something now we'd likely
step over on the street
and ignore . . .

## The House

Past midnight the house stills and wanes. Purged of the
day's mess
and loud voices. Windy shakes creak floorboards
and joists in
mass hysteria, unavoidable settle songs.

Pursed lips put forth breath sweet and tame,
in sequence stretches similar to a song sung
several years ago. Chest rises complete then falls flat.
Room warm from body heat and down pillows.
Wedged wall-side wrangled tensely in arm,
a favored toy he'd bathed with that evening.

As usual, in perch then not,
cat roams stealthily
through shadowed corners,
curtained windows, looking to pounce
on stray bugs . . . or dust balls disguised
as bugs. The wind howls through her
as she marvels at the house she doesn't
have to share tonight.

The moon casts enough light on pleasant
dreaming faces, whisper words in mind to
dance in colorful waved images often forgotten
before sleep ends. The house
too forgets and holds its walls,
a dutiful gesture to the thawing-
almost morning ground.

## The Keeper

In distance looming fear of bold to strike,
a distant gap,
cavernous cages in a corner of a loud city,
sanguine love
troubled fate
in an argument for either to exist.
I come across the man behind the gate's control.
Raise not once for me to pass
I thought him less of man but more
a keeper of things he'd not possess himself.
Nor want. Nor fear.
Just nothing.
Rows of nothing he'd keep inside himself
as the gate would rise and fall,
the arm worn but steady,
the controls gripped in shaken hand.
He'd stand slouched over
metal motion boards. Up then
down. Up then down. Watches as each
potential patient sickened him, walk calmly toward one
another, a guided harmony.

The arm up now for me in unwilling bow.
I'd further walk 'round the perimeter than test
this providence! The keeper's eyes blue-green like
balls of sea mist. Salty tears buried so deep,
eyes too dry to sleep. Yet stare
into my sex. Burning for me to change his
unchangeable mind. Callous for even the most
cruel and wasteful.

Emptied out to sea, I ran now
watching the guide grow smaller, the arm of his
gate firmly positioned at half staff. As if he's leaving
some of himself a bit more open.
In case I ever return.

## Magnolia

The grease from the radiator
left a smudge puddle in the shape
of a magnolia. Old Chevy Nova
traded for some food stamps
and a box of tools. Left idly outside
dressed in primer and a stolen plate.
A sawed off exhaust woke up two
neighbors. Mrs. Ambrose was screaming
something but I couldn't hear her above
the clamor and pops.

Magnolia puddle still pools as you work
on the rusted body. Dirty blond hair hangs
near your eyes. It's three years later. The car
runs with less pops.
It's me that clamors.

*Appeared first at* Carcinogenic Poetry.

## Morning Footprint

There's a puddle of oil in the driveway
and as it dries in the morning sun,
it takes the form of something familiar.
The neighbors hammer away while the puddle sits.
A few blocks up are sounds of power tools,
distant dog barks. Recessed children.
The breeze on the trees.

Indian summer is ending.
Colder nights rob the crickets of life.
The puddle will dry soon and keep its
shape on the driveway.
Blacker than the blacktop.
A ring takes shape around the outer layer.
It's almost tragic.
Sort of beautiful.

The footprint your car left last night.

## Opaque Box

Locked inside an opaque box;
the day we met.
Curious stares transfixed on my average body,
times when you cradled my face before we kissed,
our too-long-not-to-mean-something eye locks.
Locked away tight now,
inside the dark box so they are no longer inside me.

Then I placed in your colorful eyes,
smallish hands that ran up and down me
(in percussion like a placid petting).
Next I held, for a moment, what I thought
was your patience (it was only pity),
I stuck that way in the
back next to the playful dialogues.

For the grand finale,
I put my entire self inside!
The self that knew you,
spent time with you,
fell for you. I stuck her
in there so she can feast on you
while the other me can move on.

*In New Jersey*

I closed the lid and pushed the opaque box
into the corner of my closet.
Beside my parents' fights, adjacent from
an abortion I had when I was 18.

I then closed the closet door.
Turned out the light.
And left you there.

## Waiting for Tulips

The corner booth taken, I chose the next best place
to hide inwards. Onlookers spasm then choke on day-old
donuts. A waitress looks more like a cat than a waitress,
balances herself near the counter. Flamingo stance, tray
as a shield. Oblivious mostly, I'm the only brown-eyed
patron, in this new universe. I'm neither here sipping
coffee nor discovering a substitute for fog.
A gentleman with an olive overcoat gestures
to me if I have the time. I nod but give him nothing more.
I'm waiting for tulips.

*Appeared first at* The Momo Reader.

# THERE

## A Harmonic Gallop

A waterfall of selective adjectives
ignites and unfolds
precludes to another world at another time
like a harmonic gallop.

The story ignites a dust storm
picking up pronouns and pretense, then
freefalls into a tidal
pool.
Floating with fragmented sentences
and title phrases.

A poetic chaos.

Lip-reading while listening
like a lexis harbor.
(Expressionism
is everywhere.)
The marina lulls the buoyant boats,
as the terminology gets caught up
in the seaweed.

Terms sink fast unlike
the syllable seahorses
the next word can ride upon.

*Appeared first at* vox poetica.

## Kinda Beautiful

You're kinda beautiful.
Yes, you're imperfect,
flawed and sometimes crude.
Your hands, calloused.
Your stature, awkward.
Eyes droopy, almost sad.

Teeth misaligned and
not as bright as I'd prefer.

Your hair, often unruly,

clothes wrinkled, tattered,
musty smelled from
their basement dwelling.

Your feet are a little large for your frame.

Skin olive toned yet pale,
body hair in excess for your young age,
and you slouch a bit.

However, together all your pieces seem to fit.
Your breathy laugh, code for who gives a shit.
Taste in music is, well, a bit off the grid.
Constantly evading important questions.
Constantly reminding me of how human you are
(yeah, I forget, because to me you're not of this world).

your breath, at times, less desirable
yet your kisses are delicious.
The way we make love is not exactly "making love"
but I tell myself, after climax,
sex and love are very separate.

When we're apart and you're missed,
I realize just how much you don't make sense.
How you'd likely leave the seat up
and hardly ever compliment my wardrobe.
How I give more and take less while
you are slowly learning what being a man
is all about.

It's these things I love.
It's these exact things I find astounding.

You are kinda beautiful
just as I am kinda in love with you.


*Appeared first at* The Momo Reader *and later at* Instigatorzine.

## In Your Room

The beige-walled misshapen box we're inside.
I'm your pawn, the marionette.
My strings in your hands. My body at will.
The sun could fall from the sky and I wouldn't care,
so long as I'm in your room,
with you.

Explore me.
I'm still as stone, and wait.
Wait for only you.
Eyes closed, mouth open,
I can easily submit if you ask.
Scratch that . . . you don't have to ask.
That's why I came to your room.
To be here,
with you.

(Maybe I hope the sun falls)

## Lightning

So we were avoiding lightning,
hiding in your car but still under a very tall tree.
A bolt was on its way and it smelled of summer rain
and electric eels.
A rainbow might be coming but for now there was
just this storm and I was in the thick of it.
I wanted a cigarette but your lungs couldn't handle
it and I hated when you struggled to breathe.
Thunder vibrated the floor boards.
We had been warned.
Your hands shook a bit, and the windows fogged up
making the world outside seem that much further
away.
As the bolt hit, I felt it everywhere,
unsure if you felt it too until I saw your eyes.
Your precious rainbow eyes.
The rainbow had come so quickly.
The clouds lifted a bit then and the rumbling
got quiet and my hands shook a bit.
You picked up your finger and traced something
on the glass's condensate.
"Stay Awake, my love."
So I did.

## Orange Peel

*Peel me an orange and I'll sit down beside you*
says the girl in the purple dress
as she shuffles her feet forward.

She sways her legs awkwardly off the rail. Dirt under
fingernails, mousy brown hair hangs
over one shoulder.
She coos while watching
a sparrow dance on a dead branch below.
Her mouth turns up at the edges, pink lipped,
subtle, happy.
The smell of the orange wafts
under her nose, cute, little upturned nose.

The sun gets stuck behind a cloud,
the orange glow dulls.
She reaches out and presses her finger into
the skin.
A giggle of ha ha harmony
erupts at simple pleasure.
The orange peel falls
to the ground, her hands
cupped eager for that first
taste. I hand it over
at once, excited too,
lips pucker and pop.
*Delicious*, she squeals.

## Tiny Ball

In faith rolled up the tiny ball I carry
placed carefully, so gently, behind
lost quotations and ancient jargon
lifeless now but once abundant
pure and sane and full

dug deep down like a rabbit hole
fenced apart the dirty
grit I live in, dropped rag
dolls, limp and listless. I hide it
from you.

Then you ask and dare I answer
remain in still without a rhythm
creature calls and beckons my
arrival, climb back up and out of
darkness the tiny ball I no longer carry.

I dropped it off, at last, on your doorstep.

*Julie Ellinger Hunt*

## Playground Dads

With my hips swinging
playground whistlers
of weekend dads covered in
baseball caps and confused
limbs, arms folded then uncrossed,
then one leg, then the next
trying not to seem obvious as they
stare beneath the rim
at my ass as it walks by.
Knowing they should be
concentrating on safe play,
where-a-bouts of lil Tim and Sue
but unlike mom's head buzzing
with appointments or playdates
or what to make for dinner . . .
dad's head probably buzzes about
the game or his next jerk off
session in the shower.
Who can blame him,
he puts his business where it belongs,
left in Friday's outbox.
All thoughts slow as I walk
past, or some other MILF in
heels instead of the standard
sweat outfit and lame sneakers.

Maybe she's the nanny, he thinks.
Now erect. Tim or Sue could wait.
Play for another minute or two
while dad soaks up some imagery
for his next shower session.

*Appeared first at* Wired Ruby.

## A Cut in the Cord

A red glow in a muggy sky
now four pm on a fall day.

No need for metaphor here
the day itself has stood for enough.

The car idle at the end of a driveway
not sure if you're coming or going.

I know what I need to say
but for now, my words are impotent.

Then, like a Trojan horse, I spill
out on the ground without warning,

bits of me are everywhere and I'm exposed.
You finally see what I've contained

for so long. Rusted gears, torn bits of lingerie,
balled-up fists, tears and grit,

versions of myself, now exhausted,
worn out pages, faded and lost,

bruised body parts, bruised pieces
of fruit, bruised egos,

banished now. Away from my core.
Running to find a new place to thrive.

Hide. Live. Multiply. And now my skin
a shell; my innards, a newborn.

The cord attached. I'm looking for
somewhere to free myself, nurse myself . . .


be myself.
The cord is still attached, yet I'm free.


*Forthcoming at* vox poetica.

## Far Away

At 1:30 in the afternoon, sun streaming in
through my window, yet I sit in the dark.
Barely able to make out my own face in the nearby mirror.

You, far away, all of you, like heads
of lettuce, frilled around yourself
then rounded for a seat on soil.

Touches of earth grainy fistfuls
while pounding heart beats
sleep alone in the afternoon haze.

Flesh walls held up with a concrete
you concocted. The district doors,
now shut. Near stale people take their place.

Lie down with me, finally,
after this long day that never ends,
on the blanket I wove for this exact occasion.

Burlap overlapped with cashmere beads.
crawling beside us, the mixture of you and me,
a blending of sunbursts and afterglow.
An excuse to leave the dark.
And read letters to each other.
neat little post cards with pictures of Wyoming.

*In New Jersey*

## Train to New Orleans

On a train bound to New Orleans, she fixes her
hair just right. Cigarette-singed fingers fiddle the arm rest.
Outside her window, the scene changes quickly,
the motion blur is comforting. Her muscles relax.
Her teetering suitcase on the opposing seat packed
before sunrise. The handle taped on in a hurry.
Unaware of me, I watch her eyes well up,
wondering if she knows her bruises are showing.

Magazines reporting the latest styles piled on
my neighbor's seat. The sound of the tracks passing
beneath. A gabber on her cell phone talking about
her boyfriend's inability to commit.
The motion continues to blur.
The scenes continue to change.

She looks over as we near the station,
her tears now dry. She doesn't remember me
and that's fine. I get my cigarette ready.
The track sputtering slows. A muffled voice
announces our arrival.

We line up like ants.
Suitcase in hand, she shifts her legs
to compensate. The handle gives out
so I walk over to help her.
I reach out with my hand and she accepts me.
I carry her belongings out the door and before
we say good bye, I stick a wad of cash in her loose
jacket pocket.

## Somewhere in New Mexico

Like a parallel universe, somewhere in New Mexico,
a dust storm carries me back to you.
Floating fragments. Falling pieces.
Broken and beautiful.

The sun already set,
leaving an orange line across the cold ground.
A jackrabbit nibbles on his foot then sprints
behind a rock in lieu of the snake's return.

I'm somewhere in the sand. Half naked to only you.
Exposed flesh to only your eyes . . .
I'm somewhere next to you but no where you will see me
as the New Mexican heat gives way.

Out of sight, animals call to one another,
warning of night fears
predatory creatures that can see where they are blind.

I am blind too.

Blind to why you walk onward as I stand still.
Blind to your obvious flaws that should make me let go.
Yet I stand in the sand,
brazen to the dust storm,
always broken,
often beautiful.

Fallen pieces falling forward as you turn back,
only briefly.

*Appeared first at* The Momo Reader.

## San Francisco in November

Like a half-breed, less accepted,
with colder skin, pink with winded
days. Worried if things will show through,
shortcomings,

like an inability to see through fog,

or how the keeper fumbles with
a kiss
inside a kiss

simplicity building a steeper wall,
layered now,
hiding the mason's work.

## Key West

We take a trip to Key West
in other people's bodies.
I'm who I was ten years ago
only smarter.
You're the man you need to be
so you can accept this scenario.

We leave the snow melting
and trade up for ice cold
cocktails poolside.
We bask and talk about Faust
or the little bit we remember
about Faust.

Then pack a picnic for the beach
and make sand chairs next to sea
turtle nests.
We watch and wonder,
we wait and exchange giggles
and glances
and several awkward exchanges
before the sun kisses the
muted horizon line and I
pour sea salt on wounds
we both left too long to heal.

## Things Are OK

Georgia wasn't our favorite place.
Maybe it was the way the pollen
stuck to our cars.

The low hum from nearby buildings
whispered to pack our bags and return
home.

On the long drive, you in the U-haul,
me in the Jetta, I realized we'd be OK.
Sure we were displaced and semi-homeless
but we'd be OK.

Eight years later, Georgia is 17 hours away.
I spent the last year in bed
and you drained yourself of every last bit
so the kids were clothed and fed and happy.
The nearby houses SHOUT.
Heavy trucks empty our garbage pails.
You work.
I write.
The kids grow.

Things are OK.

## Antonym

How can you love the antonym of you,
with crystal buildings lining your perimeter,
you see through me too.
The seasons over dry land,
a crowd when I'm all alone.
A night light in the distance when the sun is
at its peak.

You laugh a bit, the overlap of my front teeth doesn't seem
to bother you, or the extra weight I now carry
(I carry loads on my back and it aches).

But seeing through me is a little less transparent
maybe. You think long and hard before a reply,
when I try to tell you,
that I am just the antonym of you.

## Along the Walls

Along the walls, I hang on.
The outskirts cushioned.
The darkness welcomed.
A shade drawn over a brick building.
Body slain, fractured, barely a body at all.
Church bells play in the distance.
Maybe there god exists.
Maybe not.

A battle cry will move me.
Something ears cannot tune out.

My body, half broken, awaits.
Awaits for something pure,
something almost divine to penetrate
brick by brick
layer by layer.
Unravel the sentimental and try to capture me bare.
See an unobstructed view,
and want more.
Not run from,
but run toward.

Not question oneself or doubt,
but let it all go for once and just breathe.

My body now a river,
homes to twists and bends
and unpredictability,
flow now. Not cold nor warm.
Just real.
And as it moves to thrust into ocean,
it brings with it something.
My body now a river.
My heart now a church.


*Appeared first at* The Momo Reader.

## Here

In a far-away place you dance with lions.
Lay under fruit-covered treetops.
Make love to a better version of me.
While I remain here, attached to a reality
you created so I'd stay away.

In your place, you can forget about me
and the dead limbs I carry.

Now . . . stuck here with my bad habits,
screwed-up outlook,
booze and occasional cigarettes,
my off-beat comments on things that hardly matter,
and the way I'd indulge the fantasy of us.

Here is just a sentiment.
An afterthought.
A way to appease myself.
There is no place I want to be,
so here is where I stay.

## You're not Here

You aren't in the framed photo
but I can almost make out
the shape of your arm in
the glass's reflection.
A white haze hangs lower
than chin level.
Maybe it's the water's mist
but I doubt it.
More likely it's a reminder
or a curse,
or even a sign that days can
stand still for as long as we
need them to.
Framed or not.

You aren't in the wind
or on the phone
or on top of the hills from
where you came from.
You aren't here or there
or anywhere in between
yet I can feel you.
I can feel you as if we're
playing the game of trust
and I'm still tilted back
into your arms' grip.

You aren't where I had found you
long ago
or was it just yesterday,
time no longer linear but
like a thousand ornaments
on a string that is twisted
into a ball, released
and then twisted again
but never in the same pattern.

You aren't my ego
or a whistle on the trees.

You, now someone entirely
different, exist somewhere
I will never be able to get to
or see,
or understand.

You aren't anywhere

you aren't even you

## Where Ever You Go

You skipped me like a stone across
the lake,
eventually sinking,
eventually disappearing.
I was eventually gone—

the moon's shadow on itself
is that part of you
or the remainder I have to live with
fractured inside a fist

or a vessel.
Treading that water,
not willing to sink
deeper as the days pile up
behind us

and we are left wondering
what's below the water line.

## Unsteady Yourself Now

The leaves uncurl just so
racing pulses ignite then slow
orange ball peeks through
as dusk's final descent gives
birth to night.

Counting sheep now sleep
heads that spun, unspin
a lapse eternal turns cold
as dreams take shape,
something takes over
when all is finally unhinged

on a hopeful breeze
with windows slightly cracked.
Knees tucked in tight
floorboards squeak while
church bells chime
as night's final descent gives
birth to dawn.

Unsteady yet calm
hands once clenched
now open.
It's time that dusk broke down.

## Accept This

As the moon accepts the dark and
lights the way,
I accept you.
Yes, our situation is a bit strange
and your habits of being alone spill over
onto mine.
What amazes me more, though,
is while I'm sifting through the twinge
you carry, I find more bright embers
to collect and keep.

Little unknown, unexplored parts hold me.
And when you think I can't notice,
I feel your hands on my face
brush my cheeks,
and your lips on my lips.
Even my teeth tingle.

Accept this, my darling,
as I accept you.

## The Storm

Small tree limb, barely a branch,
reaching out, the sky barely a blanket,
covering me.
And like the harsh elements,
you knock me about,
make me want to beg for stale air.
Boredom. A refuge.

If you're the storm, and no, I do not
wish to talk about the weather, but if
you are the ferocious storm in my life,
then just how long darkness will last
depends on you.
And your moods suck
(sorry, my dear, but they do).

Weaker than I used to be,
I wobble into bed to hide from you,
but you follow me.
Breathe me in. Hold me captive.

It's all true.
I don't want to care
or cry.
I should want to leave you behind
where you belong.
Because the storm I got through,
I survived.
The storm that taught me all about
the cold, the struggle

the storm someone else should have to weather.

## Chewing Fruit and Legumes

You made garbanzo beans
and figs
and hired a cherub to fly
above,
flap her wings,
and make perfect shadow
dances on concrete.
You pulled the figs apart
holding their weightiness
in large palms,
the heat from sun
and breath
and beans
fogged your glasses up.
"Chewing Fruit and Legumes,"
you said, would
make a perfect poem.
The cherub dove
down and snatched
your glasses from your face,
then a fig,
then a kiss.

*In New Jersey*

I just giggled and
asked the cabana boy
for another drink.
And another hour
with you in this silly dream
that makes me smile.


*Appeared first at* vox poetica.

## In My Mind

In my mind, I drive past your house three
times a week. I whisper in your ear while
you sleep to forgive me and love me again.
And you obey.
We slow dance after a dusk time picnic
in your yard
while the dogs play together
and my biggest worry is nowhere near me.

In my mind, you are still you but you're a better
version. You're kinder and see me as I am.
This time I love you, but not so much that it hurts.
I get lost in your eyes but not for as
long, and not as deeply.

I get lost . . . just enough.

And we laugh more so I can
see your silly smile, watch your
eyebrows dance. Fall in love over
and over and over again with those
rainbow eyes framed with black lashes.
I have missed those eyes locked on mine.

In my mind, we are still together somehow,
two versions of ourselves,
while the real copies pretend they are still angry.
These two creatures kiss for hours . . .
totally,
entwined,
elated . . .
and perfectly matched.

## Incapable

Some are incapable of love,
Disguised as folly. Pin-tucked. Over cooked.
Thrown down into a barrel and aged for years.
(Over ripe. Over seasoned . . . Over looked)

And only fruit flies come near, left to rot on the counter,
in the sun. Away from life.
Away from things that matter.
Most are incapable of love.
As most are incapable of fear.
Dare to really put oneself out there, to really be afraid,
bold, naked . . . on the line.

Incapable of running after something that is merely
a few feet ahead.
To stand by someone and watch time
pass on their face and not look away.
Not want to look away.

We are all incapable of something.
Just as we are all capable of everything.
If only we'd stop searching . . .
and see what's been there all along.

**I can save you:**

> Just before you
> think you're
> over-filled
> and only the deepest
> cave could hold you,
> let me try to cup my hands
> around the woes
> and drink your pain.

*In New Jersey*

# SOMEWHERE ELSE

## Someplace Else

Far away where hearts
still beat but mend quickly
twined in bough a small
nest gives life to love
not flight
where "what" and "if"
never meet
and things we hold
inside from fear
are read on lips
as easy as words
are spewed.

On a spot sun can
beat down and not
harm, radiate but not
burn. Children can play
outside and be
safe.

And to suffer is purely
poetic. That is some
place else I'd like to be.

Where a rainbow comes
before a downpour
and casts the colors in your
eyes just for me.

Julie Ellinger Hunt

Where the smell of autumn
lasts through winter's tiny
days, and winter nights
are only cold enough . . .
Prayers are listened to
and weighed . . . maybe even
answered now and then.

In small hands where
wonders never cease
and grown men can
cry on public streets
and my heart can leap
and not fear death, depth,
or height. Where tomorrow
can wait as each day is
lived thoroughly, patiently,
and plentiful.

Where love is not hearts
and flowers but life itself.

This is some place I'd rather be.

Where I can lay my head down
each night without regret,
without ponder or doubt,
without self sacrifice
or the waging war that
burns my bones and singes
my fingertips each time
I reach out to touch someone.

*In New Jersey*

Where I can sing sweetly,
freely, gracefully
the tune in my head,
your tune.

Where *hope* and *faith*
are not two silly words
painted on signs but rather
real, concrete things I
can fathom.

Where the stars align
just right and sparkle
just so.

Where the last words I write
are just the beginning . . .

This is some place I look to be.


*Appeared first at* Rafter.

## Can I Drink You Away

Can I drink you away . . .
sip each smile we shared, each
time our hands touched and I felt that
zing. I loved that zing. (I probably
loved you. And you probably
know that.)
>            I want to gulp each kiss,
>            waste away our significant
>            eye locks. (Those eye locks are why
>            I'm writing this!)
Drunken stupor won't wipe you away,
put you way back in the memory bank
beside my first skinned knee. Way back
where I need you to be . . . at least for now.

Can I wish you away . . .
next eyelash that falls I'll try
my best to blow you away
as far as I can. Will it work,
will this pain get better soon
or will I spin so far out of my
own body that I'm no longer
me?

## Pattern

When I'm out of words where do I go . . .
You aren't here. My legs are numb and unforgiving.
Like I've walked across the Garden State to find you.
Instead, I'm likely chasing my own tail in a peculiar pattern.
Maybe that's how crop circles are formed instead of a
mass conspiracy.

The beer on tap is stale, the patrons bitter.
No one is allowed to smoke and drink like leeches. We all have
to behave in this pattern. An assumed pattern
conformed to by most. It is a mass conspiracy . . .

So what if I want to drink and smoke and screw
'til my body gives out, then sleep for a decade.
That statement deserved an exclamation point
but I didn't have the energy to exclaim it.

I adhere to the pattern I'm expected to adhere to.
Awaken. Produce. Stay busy. Say little. Keep head down. Sleep.
Days are divided into six increments.
I wait for you in between.
Time slivered out just for the pathetic ritual.
You aren't coming to pick me up or save me.
You'll leave me in this pattern
because that is what is expected of you too.

## Carcass

Diseased and rotting, limbed branch
jets out, scratches
walkers as they stroll by.
You're the over active wind
that will eventually snap me and
I'll fall parallel to the dirt and stones—

probably trip a well suited hiker as he walks up the path.

Diseased and rotting,
internal limbed branches,
the relationship carcass,
bones passed on as months pass me.
No longer the wind that
will knock me over,
I bury your face next to the neighbor's
willow tree. A shallow plot
for your shallow affection.

Probably missed only by me only because I value trivial things.

The bones of us deteriorate.
Yours in dirt. Mine exposed with
whiter flesh, still diseased,
still rotting, but finally beautiful.

Soon to become a bronzed replica
I display on a shelf above the toilet.


*Appeared first at* vox poetica.

## Dungeon

I entered the dungeon
brighter than a dungeon ought to be
listening to the hums of a rainbow beetle
clenched fists birth the last mediocre morning.

Swiftly I run toward the light you offered once
hoping it hasn't burned out, feet in trot,
coming calmly closer, not sure if it's the echo
of myself or new steps.

So I hug a wet wall, slippery cement bricks
hold me up. I'm conscious of everything.
I see in mosaic. My world now tiled completely
over by his. Pink hues dance with orange, blackened
a bit in corners where critters wait.

*I know you live alone and want it to remain so*
*but I'm here and can't leave so come and see me,*
I think. The wet wall drips. I hear the water falling.
I don't want to be alone anymore. I want to scream
for you. Brown-eyed warrior.

You will not hear me. Why I know but it's still unfair
as I have lived my life up 'til now out of your way,
while there is still little peace and you know I don't
belong! I reach for you again to touch your tiled face.
Closed before, I open only for you.

Let me remain open.

_*Julie Ellinger Hunt*

## If words could heal and I could write . . .

I took the dress off you made me. It was pretty but
not my fondest color. I'm better wearing my real self,
one person no one would want to know. Hah, my real
self. I'm always hiding anyway.

The dress, sporting perfectly formed purple daisies,
is balled up now on your floor. I bet you'd rather look
at it than me. Who blames you. This isn't about angst
or anger or spite. It's not a poem telling anyone off
or betting for a realization that will very likely never
come to fruition.

No, this is not a poem about love either. Or mourning
or death. Or life. Or the meaning of it all. It's just words
on a page I composed to take my mind off of myself for
a few minutes.

My overwhelming, worried mind. Ugh. I wish I could just
turn it off! Numb myself. I drank the last bit of wine and I
can still feel my ache. Not much makes sense these days
as they blur into each other.

____
____
_____
_____

A blur of mornings, alcohol, missing you and missed meals.
A blur of tears and distractions, and wishes of things I'll never
find or have or hold. I blur into you for a moment and it feels
nice. I hate the word "nice" but that's how it feels. Nicer than
most things feel lately.

Butane lighter in hand, I want that dress to burn. Purple to black,
then smoke, then nothing . . . fade away like you fade from me as
you
read my pathetic attempt to smile. Half happy I'm with you.
Half numbed. I say good-bye again but this time you will let me
go. Fight me less, I beg. Fight for me more. The dress you made
now empty of me as I leave in just my skin.

## In the Desert

In the desert, I'd run to you,
under a petrified tree or a rock mountain,
under the darkest blanket of sky and stars,
your feet planted in red sands and my hands
holding my hair back as the desert wind blows.

We'd lay on a thrift store quilt, its color wouldn't
matter, but it would be soft and forgiving as I nestled
into the crook of your neck. Your skin would be warm and
sun kissed and smell of cactus flower. You'd sing to me
and I'd close my eyes every chance I had to take it all in,
knowing time would quickly pass and we'd have to rejoin
civilization.

For dinner, you'd make a fire and treat me to the finest meal.
The blaze would highlight the dimples that hide under your beard
and I too would think of how far the city should stay.
Side by side, we'd read. You'd choose something by Bukowski and I'd
consider something less urban, maybe Jack London or Thoreau.

Sleep would come eventually. I'd be afraid of distant howls of course,
and continue to nudge you each time your breathing slowed. You'd insist
you were awake when dreams rushed in . . . I'd nestle closer, tighter in
the place I most like to be.

*In New Jersey*

And as we drove away, and left behind our imprint in the sand,
you'd promise we'd return . . .
and I'd say it didn't matter, so long as
we could always have this memory . . .
and then you'd retort,
"That's what memories are, my darling."

*Appeared first at* Wired Ruby.

## My Story Left Me

It left me again.
Escaped for a stint at a hole-in-the-wall bar.
I was white knuckled but it still got away.
I even chased it for a while
and grabbed it by the tale . . .

While running it lost part of my alphabet.
I ran behind it
(with a bag in one hand
and lexicon in the other).
As luck would have it, the tale was quite shrewd

and disintegrated in hold.
Chameleon spots that came back
together once my hand retreated,
a glossary gimmick,
it hated to be cornered.

So I changed my game up.
Sat on a bar stool with a pint of
Guinness, knowing good and well the encyclopedia
serving my drinks had selective perception.
I wasn't nearly as worldly as he.

I lit my last cigarette, smoky syllables filled
the air around me. Tempted to finish the
drink too fast before my story was ready.
Its sweet barley malts swirl around the glass
while I use my last-page-energy, coy
fragility. If I remain still and submissive
my story may follow me.
So I leave it at last,
my own tale
miles behind, I grow closer to home.

## Ode to Tumbleweed

In my dreams, the desert is never quite so dry.
The cowboy I make love to every Thursday holds
a steady 9 to 5 on Wall Street. His burly hands
can pour whiskey and fiddle on a keyboard
just as nice.
His chaps, always modest like his
devotion to tumbleweeds he flocks
to every Thursday in my bed.

My body sanguine to his charm,
the tilt of his hat,
his *yes ma'ams*,
the curl of his pronounced upper lip,
and how he drinks his whiskey neat
(he always "cowboys-up" while I have my drink
on the rocks . . . ).
We make love in the red satin sand as a coyote
sings its tune.

Whiskey tongue tastes
my urban kiss. I hold back some as a
tumbleweed dances past.
*It's lovely here*, I whisper
to the starry sky and the Manhattan
cowboy. *Yes ma'am*, he says.

*Appeared first at* Calamity Jane.

## Rip Current

Like a rip current in the middle of aesthetic pleasure,
a violent beauty calling out, destructive ambivalence.

Capsized, turned inward, looking at the self I avoid,
blindly inching forward to the reflection on mirrored glass.

Time has run out for us. The eye of the storm now past.
Wobbling still, I make my way to dry land. There's a light
house in the distance. I see it. I focus on it. I call to it in my mind.
The ocean picking up bits I cast off of myself. Bits I don't want back.

The tide coming in brings me back. It wants me reconnected.

## Things Come Together

The breeze picks up at the end of
an Indian summer day.

A poem begins with you. And ends with me.

The hand cupped as water flows.

Planets begin to align.

The car idles as I plan my escape.

The voices calmer in the morning hours.

Stones skip on top of a creek,
leap, then sink out of sight.

The squirrels chase each other up a tree
just as the dog makes his rounds.

A child  squeals with the afternoon sun,
walking hand in hand with her mother.

*In New Jersey*

And as we lingered a little longer,
you looked to me for answers you knew I didn't have.

Since it's true, some things do come together . . .
a kiss . . . a lightning strike . . .

But how long they will stay together,
we can really never know.
What may matter is how long we can try.

## City Street

The street ends.
A chambermaid runs from the rain,
ducks into the Flea Bag Motel.
A taxi's signal pops . . . blink blink . . . pops.

Stretched along the avenue
a video store welcomes a customer once
an hour. High-heeled bar whores stand
around, wait for happy hour cocktail prices.

Puppy dog eyed blonde child safe under
a bus stop structure. She sits while mother
gets misted by dirty rain castoffs from passing cars.
A horn blows as one car catches a peek at her exposed legs.

Check cashers work diligently to rip off as many
people as they can before closing time. A wino
pushes his cart with the singing wheel up behind
the abandoned warehouse.

I crouch low in my seat. Coffee steam warmth close
to nose hairs. Pen ink runs a little dry. I press
the point to my tongue but it does little.
I have to end this.

As the city never ends. My city. All I got
is 65 cents, some words and observation.
A faded half decent poem scribbled on a
napkin.

*Appeared first at* Caper Literary Journal.

## New York Lion

*(inspired by Charles Bukowski's* the tabby cat*)*

The street vendors are hiding.
Here comes the Lion now.
Prowess. Proud. Full of himself.
A low engine hiss and then a thump.
Thumping on sparkly pavement
down 8th Avenue, red exhaust circles
tourists. The tourists just stare, wide
eyed, jaws drooping.
Forgotten camera clicks.

^ up look up ^
Monstrous clouds cover crowded building tops.
Tiny windows hide.
Lion loops, then lowers,
scoops his first victim into his hands.
Pleased with his choice, he licks his lips.
The locals cheer, half scared out of their wits,
half relieved it wasn't them.
Fear from another airplane maybe.

A dirty Rastafarian drums prey beats.
41st and 42nd Streets spill onto Port Authority's
front walk. The Lion just waits.
In Yiddish he kvetches something irrelevant.
On-lookers applaud him as he bows.

**What Love IS:**

On the floor lies a basin,
the basin holds the left-over bath water,
the water holds the remains,
and it goes on until the smallest particle
is split in two and there is no more.

On the table sits a glass jar,
unremarkable and without purpose.
It isn't filled with anything perishable or non-
perishable.
It isn't filled with anything but air and glass
and shimmer.

On the wall hangs a grayish square
where the picture used to be,
or maybe a door,
whatever it was that took up the spot on the wall
that is now bare
and shines brighter than the rest.

*Appeared first at* Wired Ruby.

## You can be my cherry

Connected by the stem
we are,
or were, long ago,
maybe in a castle on the
Aegean Sea,
or in a cabin burning pellet
fires
by a lake,
in the Adirondacks.
Duck calls
or war cries
doesn't matter
not the backdrop
not the noises
but the quilt
that stitched us together,
stem to stem
cherry neighbors,
or we're just two silly
lost freaks
that finally found
each other.


*Appeared first at* Wired Ruby.

## I Lost Myself

I lost myself three years ago.
Maybe I went where the socks end up,
far away from their specific mate.
Or maybe I took myself off the grid
for a while like a backpacker wandering
around Europe, trying to discover something
meaningful. Wherever I went, I'm not "here"
anymore. Now this person with my name
and face is not me at all. I wear a mask
that looks a lot like me, sure. But it
definitely isn't me.
You can tell by the edges of skin flapped
over. It's unraveling
quickly, unfurling as fast as seconds pass.
I think I went for a detour of sorts
back behind cheerful mountain tops
and kissing cherubs.
Way far back, like to the edges where
hawks don't even want to fly to
even when there is easy prey. Rows of frozen,
fatty mice with the sweetest meat.
Maybe it's like the old tale of the world
being on the turtle shell's back and I'm
somewhere inside a green groove,
nestled on a slow-moving pseudo reptile,
pseudo fable.
Wherever I ended up I hope I'm smiling
more and thinking of bullshit less. Maybe
my mind has finally stopped its retarded

churning—wasting thoughts on things
that hardly matter. I hope my legs
are thinner and longer and my
home is a bit less chaotic. Maybe
I am living near a brook that makes
the perfect bubbling noises so I
am soothed to sleep each night
I keep my window open.
Ha, wouldn't it be fantastic
if my neighbor was the ideal muse
and I could be inspired for days
without sleep, forced
to create masterpiece after masterpiece.
I hope I have an elaborate plan too where
everything has its time and place. Laughter
comes after the joke is told. Crying is done
properly after something truly tragic
or at the end of a touching film.
The streets are paved perfectly smooth
and all the signs use a larger font so they
are not misread.
Even food is audacious. Spices richer. Juices
delectable. And kisses can last as long as they
want to. They're not cut short by a race to
the next event.
My hair grows without a single dead end.
Oh, and I receive a paycheck for being
productive after hours.
Intoxication isn't so taboo.
Sex neither.

People don't have to give a fuck about doing
what feels good.
Dogs chase their tails as much as they'd like without
looking foolish.
Children can play outside way past dusk and
don't have to bother wearing a helmet because
bikes do not tip over.
Birthday cake is not just for birthdays.
And I can sit as close to the TV as I'd like!

If I'm ever found, I hope I look surprised
like the dumb people who are about to
receive a gigantic check at their front
door.
Like I had no idea I was lost to begin with.
My disappearance wasn't my doing at all
and I tried really hard to come back
but couldn't find my way? Yes! And it was
believable. No one would roll their eyes
when I told them the story of my trip
home. They'd applaud at the finish
and pat me on the back for a job
well done. Having the guts to come
back in the first place. And then we'd
all laugh like it was a big misunderstanding.

Until then, wherever I am, I hope I'm ok.
I'll settle for being just alright. Just existing
somewhere. And this stranger that looks a lot
like me has only abducted me for a short
while, and it really isn't such a big deal.

## A Walk

He runs down a sloped road,
toward me, jeans too big for his frame,
so one hand holds them up slightly.
I'm embraced then released.
Intoxicated, I lean as I walk beside him.
The sloped road continues to slope
and we eventually come to the dark edge
of a street. Something scurries by. I'm unsure so
he takes my hand. "Don't worry," he whispers.
I nod. And we walk on.

## I love it when you kiss me

I love it when you kiss me, crazy lips
take me someplace new each time.
Like a new pair of shoes without having
the discomfort of breaking them in,
your lips always fit mine quite well.
we get to jump through time to
different places. Your lips, a portal,
your hands, an excursion,
explore me all you want.

I love it when you kiss me, neck hairs
stand straight up, goose bumps ravage
my skin. My legs go limp, my ears ring.
I'm inebriated, drunk from your taste,
touch, smell. I feel you everywhere,
places I can't say aloud. You thrill me
like no other. Touch. Turn. Tantalize.
Tease. My long hair waved down my
back, you brush aside so you may
better see my expression. The
ecstasy you make me wear all
over. As you kiss me all over.

I love it when you kiss me, sanguine
tongue. See me over and over mouth
your name. I call to you and you just
stare, transfixed, content, eager to
make me feel more. Eyes roll back
in earnest. Back arched, teeth clenched.
Your body kisses my body. We dance
and I'm like your mirror, opposing sides
in perfect sync. A ritual compliment.
Oh, how I love it when you kiss me!

*Julie Ellinger Hunt*

## My Onion

I can love you like no other because you're like
this onion I have peeled over and over in  my head
and in front of my face. Your layers are messy.
You make my eyes burn. You often make me cry.
You add some flavor to mundane days—yet at times
                              I'm left with an ache in my stomach.

Hardly sweet, you often sting me in your raw form.
And if I love you still, knowing this, having tasted
your imperfections, flaws, intensities,
obtuse angles,
hunger for purity,
discovery,
the truth, pursued to extremes,
the oddities you love, the commonness you reject,
the road you will always travel—longer, bumpier,
covered in glass shard gravel that rips at the soles of your feet
and everyone's flesh that dares to walk beside you,
your doubts of humanity (who can blame you),
the smile that plays peek-a-boo.
Wide-eyed, you were always able to look inside me.
Not at me or above me or beyond me.

Locked, we'd stare. How can that connection,
even as an onion layer, not convince you?
Purple skinned or not, fawn flakes,
or amber crust.
I can handle you and love you like no other.
Most others would detest your layers,
while I revel in them.
I match one layer with my own.
Your beauty in just that,
the complication.

Julie Ellinger Hunt

## who am i

1.

I'm a black hole
a good excuse
a reservoir
I'm the very thing you prayed for
the opposite of why you cringe
a pleasurable escape
a place to lay your head
I'm a tool belt
I offer many things
I can fix mistakes you make
or repair the flaws you'll most likely
make tomorrow.

2.

the car hisses and then stops
I'm the reason it rolls over
I'm nonetheless and
none the weaker
I'm exactly why your car starts up again
after leaving the door ajar all night.

3.

tucked deep in pockets,
left inside
through the delicate cycle you
favor then scorched on high heat
like a squished-up dollar bill ball

4.

Growing tired now
weaker, I'm the thing that holds you together.
A dried-out pine cone,
stiff and segmented.

Arranged in similar layers.
The breeze won't move me.
Your words won't affect me.

I am here.
I am isolation.
I am me.

## I Purge the Springtime

On this page, I purge you.
I let go of your weak conversation.
One-word answers to intricate quizzes.
I expel your habit of lumping me in with other women
as if I was hardly special enough to stand on my own.
I assume you're more of an addiction than the
"real thing." So I purge every sweet word I shared
and try to reverse any compliment you retained.
I let go of your solitude and the wall you hold up and
the friends you share more with and the time you
take to read my thoughts on a page and choose not
to reply.

On this page, I purge myself. The part of me that
still gives a damn about you.
The part I want surgically removed from the rest of me.
The "me" that misses you, misses your kisses, your
eyes locked on mine.
I scroll on this page for the world to see, the
very essence of what makes me want any part of you
since you let me go long before I could.
And I still hold on and check to see if you care,
maybe read between the words you don't share anyway.

On this page, I try to heal.
Mend myself of the hole your leaving has put in its place,
finally listening to the dozens of times you tried to say:
it's over and I chose not to listen.

## Bored of You

A few weeks ago, we'd be talking
about bad song lyrics or how it's
impossible for a watermelon to be a vegetable.

I'd make fun of your pigeon-toed stride or
the way you'd trim your beard and forget
about your bushy nose hairs.

You might say something like "God seekers
suck the life out of humanity," and I'd roll
my eyes.

Yet today you're gone and I don't care to
write about you any longer. My pieces were
already scattered about, you only kicked

them further away. A fine accomplishment
but now I'm bored of pining. Instead I think
I'll write something about God seekers and how
harmless they are.

## Tired Eyes

If tired eyes could see
the world as it ticks
and stews and moves
in bedrooms where babies
sleep, their dreams
labyrinths to further days

where we can weep for time
and space and wishes spent
flying through air—
albino dandelion
fuzz floating
as hopeful girls
twirl and blow
with dresses spinning
and air scented
perfectly.

If tired eyes could see,
they'd look for Paris
folded in a paper napkin
or an electric eel as purple
as my veins beneath my skin.

They'd look for calm
in crowded streets
or content worn on serious
faces.

*In New Jersey*

Glasses full of wine
just the right shade of blush
as my cheeks blush for you.

And finally as the world
would end, tired eyes
could close and see behind
the lids
balanced remains of simplicity
and acceptance.


*Forthcoming at* Ascent Aspirations.

## With an Arrogant Lover

Loosely, I fell in love with you.
Or was it you who fell for me,
the me you
thought you saw
sitting on the bench below an angry sky.
As it erupts over again, you erupt for me . . .
turned inside out from being overseas too long.
Brackish water tides clean up
our mess
in a drenched symphony.

We used to walk hand in hand in my head.
The store fronts jealous.
You'd recite the Vietnamese menu, and
I'd sing about the dandelions being weeds,
unfairly so.

As dusk came to town, we'd find a hide-away
in a laundromat.
The swishes and swirls
a new back-up singing group.

*In New Jersey*

If the town allowed it we'd
paint only the good parts red,
while dressed up in my grandmother's pearls,
and you wearing the itchy wool overcoat
loosely buttoned.

Chinatown merchants scatter sawdust
and rice patties. We peek into the vacant
theater to make sure it's still playing our show.

I bow to your hand as you kiss the air,
aware of your loose lips
on loose love.

You're the only arrogant lover in my city tonight.


*Appeared first at* Ascent Aspirations.

**Dear Sir:**

I decided to express myself in a letter so I do not offend you with sentimental form. It is my regret to notify you of my unhappiness. While I strongly appreciate your efforts (if much has been made), I am still quite sick of being miserable.

Because I'm aware of your intelligence and diligence toward things you value as important, I'm appalled by your indecent forgetfulness. Your departure is always premature. And arrival, well, that is yet to be determined. Are you ever really present anyway?

Sure, it is likely that my constant doting has skewed my perception. But in all fairness, it is you that cannot let go of me. Technically, promises have yet to be broken, but, still, not enough of them have been made.

Enclosed with this letter I include a fracture of myself. A tiny splinter. Just the teeny bit you chipped away. You're welcome to keep it as a souvenir. Maybe you can put it next to the semi-awful manuscript you've yet to submit.

Sincerely,
The Sick-of-Your-Shit chick

*Appeared first at* Wired Ruby.

## See Ya

The moon hung a little lower so I took it as a sign.
Thrusts onto garbage heaps—
dazzling like a flickering flashlight
at the edge of a dying battery.
Liquefied some remains and placed them in a jar.
The large pickle jar from your collection.
I doubt you'll miss it.

All thumbs, my last attempt to write you a note
saying goodbye.
A farewell more to your apartment,
cat,
and collection of old forty-fives.

**Julie Ellinger Hunt** lives in Northwest New Jersey. After completing her education at the University of Delaware, Hunt went on to publish her poetry in more than 20 journals internationally. Her off-beat, gritty style fused with sentiment and surreal observation is well received by the community. Her first book, *Ever Changing* (Publish America, 2010), was well regarded by fellow writers and happy readers. She hopes to continue to grow as a writer and contribute as much as possible while living under the same roof with her two sons and husband (she speculates they may be part alien). Keep up with her at http://jthunt.wordpress.com/.

www.ingramcontent.com/pod-product-compliance
Lightning Source LLC
Chambersburg PA
CBHW051729090426
42738CB00010B/2157